I0470326

SO, YOU WANNA BE A LAWYER AT A BIG LAW FIRM?

What you need to know about practicing law at a big firm before going to law school or before taking that job offer

JULIA BENICE, ESQ.

This is a work of nonfiction. Names, identities and certain circumstances have been changed to protect the privacy and anonymity of the various individuals portrayed.

Copyright © 2011 Julia Benice, Esq.
All rights reserved.

ISBN: 1453824766
ISBN-13: 9781453824764

TABLE OF CONTENTS

For My Parents

ACKNOWLEDGMENTS

There are many people I would like to thank for making this book possible.

I would like to thank Paul DiLisi, Cherise Wolas and Mona Yunan for their input on my earliest drafts. Special thanks to Griffin Broadway, who, pen in hand, gave me a great in-depth critique of my work.

I would like to thank my husband, who knows the first paragraph of my very first draft all too well. And, last, but not least, thank you to my parents for seeing me through those law firm days.

INTRODUCTION

To Go or Not To Go to Law School?

Why go to law school? There are certainly many different reasons—all good—why you might want to make that move. But the idealized image of lawyers presented in blockbuster movies and popular TV shows is not among them. *Law and Order*, *The Practice*, *LA Law*, *Boston Legal*, *Legally Blonde* and *A Few Good Men* entertain viewers with a glamorized picture of the practice of law and are, in the end, *fiction*. The reality of the work and politics, especially at a large law firm, is something quite different. I suspect that, if shows like these were to reveal what really happens in firms, the networks would be out of business, and there would be just a handful of lawyers in this country today, instead of more than 1,000,000.[1]

Without realty TV as a resource, *So, You Wanna Be a Lawyer at a Big Law Firm?* is your best reference tool, especially if you are already a practicing attorney and think you would like to make the move to a big firm,[2] if you are already in law school and are seriously contemplating a job at a large firm, or if you are considering going to law school for the purpose of working at a major firm.

Although this book primarily focuses on major law firms, in some sections I make reference to small firm practice and public service law for points of illustration and contrast to big firm practices. Reading this book will provide you with crucial information and first-hand insights into law firm life and will be a critical part of your research before you decide to work at a big law firm or attend law school in order to work at a major law firm, and will enable you to make an informed decision about whether to take the plunge.

My decision to go to law school was based on several factors. I had graduated from college with a B.A. in the history of art. Although I enjoyed learning about art history, I realized that I was not passionate enough about it to devote another ten years of my life studying for a Ph.D. and writing the dissertation that would be required if I were going to do anything serious in the field. A master's degree was not a good option for me since only forty-five percent of those receiving Ph.D.s in any academic field were employable in the mid-nineties. I had to think about my future and how I was going to make a living while, at the same time, doing something that I liked. To me, security was a big issue, and I wanted something reliable and dependable.

After considerable thought, I decided on law school. It was the most logical step, as I did not know exactly what I wanted to do with my life. After all, I was a decent student, so law school wouldn't be that difficult. And I would come out with the ability to make a good living—and to do some good at the same time. In addition, I had heard that you could do anything with a law degree.

So I made the decision to go to law school and got accepted to Columbia University. Of course, a law degree was just the beginning of the rest of my career. It was only once I was attending law school that I began making choices about the next step: work. In hindsight, I really didn't make a conscious decision about what I wanted to do with my law degree or the job I wanted once I graduated. It was more like I was a part of a herd—being prodded along in one direction. Columbia didn't so much change my perspective on things as it molded and created a perspective *for* me.

With heavy recruitment from top law firms in and around New York City, I was easily lured into the idea of working at a prestigious law firm. It was as if there were no other options. Besides, I needed to make substantial money with all my law school debt, and the firms offered the only realistic possibility of getting out of debt in a reasonable period of time. It seemed like my work life was neatly laid out for me. I would not only gain experience at a big firm, but also earn a lot of money, even doing pro-bono work. I was especially thrilled after experiencing the summer program at one of New York's major firms.

As a summer associate, my work was varied and interesting. I worked on litigation matters, doing research and writing for partners who needed legal issues threshed out. I also worked on corporate matters, revising a myriad of agreements under the detailed instruction of senior associates. I enjoyed the work, and, more importantly, I received positive feedback about my performance and ended up with an offer at the end of the summer. I was extremely happy—relieved—that I was assured a job after graduating law school. I was especially elated to be working at such a congenial firm that I felt I could call home, and where one day I might even make partner. I thought that anything was possible.

What happened after graduating law school while working at several major firms is what led me to write this book. It was a reality check for me, and I thought I should share my experiences with others who might be in danger of making the same mistakes.

That's how this book was born. I hope that this candid presentation of my trials and tribulations—and those of my friends and colleagues—might help others to make more informed decisions about whether to attend law school, and whether working in a major law firm will really fulfill their dreams.

CHAPTER ONE

A Snapshot of Law Firm Life

I got into a top-five law school! How proud of myself I was, and how proud my parents were. I wouldn't have to worry about making a measly $30,000 a year and being treated like a second-class citizen. My future was secure. I would start out making at least $160,000. WOW. And law school? What a cinch for me; after all, I've been an excellent student my whole life.

Law School

Law school was great. Well—after the first semester, anyway. I loved going to classes, and I liked research and writing. Best of all, though, I loved the non-scheduled schedule: I could study when I wanted to, and I had time to exercise and hang out with my new friends.

But being a student again was just a step toward something else: actually being a lawyer. What *kind* of lawyer did I want to be? I really didn't know. The question didn't bother me, though; it seemed like something that would work itself out. Columbia had already set up interview schedules with all the top law firms. I figured I would just go to the interviews and see what emerged. In any case, working for any of these firms would give me options: While I was gaining valuable experience in the practice of law, I could pay down my debt and learn how to be a lawyer. Meanwhile, I would be making business connections that could allow me to move into the business world, if I were to decide to go in that direction. It didn't matter that I didn't know much about what corporate attorneys did. I mean, a lawyer is a lawyer, right? How bad could it be? Besides—as a summer associate, I would get to learn all I needed about what the life of a corporate attorney was all about. Or so I thought.

The Bait and Switch

And ye shall know the truth, and the truth shall make you free.
—John 8:32

As a summer associate, I never had it so good. Everything was fantastic: Three-hour lunches four days a week with mile-high desserts (my personal favorite), and elegant dinners at least twice a week! Oh—and the baseball games, concerts, theater tickets, massages, and other summer events. Who ever thought work could be so much fun! Best of all, I got paid $3,000 a week. I thought life was good. And I didn't even have to work so hard. Sure, I had research assignments and short drafting assignments, but the work was not grueling and didn't take much time to complete. I was beginning to think that working at a firm was not going to be as difficult as I worried it might be.

I was never so wrong in my life.

One Year Later: A Day in the Life of a First-Year Real Estate Associate . . .

7:30 a.m. After hitting the snooze about seven times, I lie in bed staring at the ceiling trying to convince myself that today will be a good day. I eventually make my way out of bed to the shower, and by the time I've stepped out, the shower has awakened me. But there's not much it can do to get me ready for the stress of the day ahead. A half-hour after lifting the covers of my cocoon, I'm out the door.

Another sardine-packed subway in NYC will get me to work *almost* on time, my stress levels ever increasing. I can't relax as details of the day run every which way in my head. I've long forgotten about attempting to read the paper or a novel on the train. I have my own thoughts and the rush of people to box me in. I can't concentrate on anything other than the tortuous day ahead. At last, after two transfers, I've reached my final destination. But coffee first—of course.

Ahhh, Starbucks. I will not forego my double-shot skim latte. I don't care if I'm late. I was in the office until 1:30 a.m., and I'll be damned if I won't treat myself right before the start of my new miserable day. Oh, yeah, today will be a great day, right? I forgot. Besides, what's $3.48 anyway?

Latte in hand, I get off on the 13th floor at 9:30 a.m. I am not superstitious, but now that I think of it, buildings are not supposed to have a 13th floor. I should have known right from the day I accepted the job offer that this was going to be a curse. I finally make it to my office. No "Hello" to or from anyone—except my secretary, Linda; she's the only one with any courtesy. The attorneys are wandering about like characters in *Night of the Living Dead:* no energy, no desire for interaction, certainly no desire to say, "Good Morning."

My office is barren—except for my $200,000 diplomas on the wall and the files strewn about the desk and floor. Yes, I'm ready for a great day! I glance at the long list of e-mails. I haven't deleted any since I turned on my computer eleven months ago. The truth be told: I've never even bothered to read all that firm-related stuff about this rule and that one. I don't have the *time* to read any of that; if it's really that important, they'll track me down. It's not like they won't be able to find me. I *live* here now! I see nothing of importance in the e-mail list, so I briskly move on to the next task.

I've got to proofread all of my revisions from the night before. Of course, I find many mistakes. So I mark-up the documents (about nine in all) and hand them to Linda to revise. Linda can't help me, though, because she's working on something for her *real* boss—a partner (who happens to be my boss, as well). We'll call him "Partner No. 1." His work takes precedence. Of course.

Plan B: I tell myself that I can revise my own documents and fit this into my schedule. Okay, I'll do this first and just put off my review of title and survey 'til a little later. Not being a very good typist (no one ever told me lawyers should know how to type), it takes me a couple of hours of revising, printing, proofing, and revising again. Finally, when my documents are completed, I run blacklines, which show the comparison of the latest version against the previous one. This task adds about another half-hour. I rid myself of these documents by handing them over to Partner No. 1. Perfect—just in time for lunch. But I still haven't gotten to the title and survey I wanted to review. I'll get to it right after lunch.

Anxious for the break, and needing to re-fuel if I'm going to make it through another marathon day, I head down to the cafeteria four floors below. (Lucky me—I never have to leave the building!) En route, another partner (Partner No. 2) intercepts me. He needs a printout of a mortgage I worked on last week, and he needs it *now*. I wrack my brain trying to remember what the hell he's talking about: I worked on a mortgage last week? Jeez, I don't remember; it all seems the same to me! *Think, think, think!* I finally figure it out—not because of my foolproof memory, but because of the database. Thank God for technology! What a fool I would have looked like if I had to ask him, "Mortgage? What mortgage?"

I run it over to his office because twenty minutes of searching is just too long for him to wait. But he doesn't want to see it. He wants me to send it to the client, along with blacklines of prior drafts. Maybe Linda can help me now?

Of course not. She's still working on Partner No. 1's documents, and she'll be tied up for the rest of the day. *Shit!* I quickly review the mortgage again to make sure there are no typos. Of course, there are. I make revisions. Then I blackline it against the first draft of the mortgage. Then I draft an e-mail to the client, including clean and blackline drafts of the mortgage, and copy it to Partner No. 2. Whew! That's off my plate. And it only took 54 minutes.

What time is it now? 1:30 p.m. How did *that* happen? I still haven't gotten around to the task that was supposed to be first today: that title and survey project. The phone rings. It's another partner (Partner No. 3) calling about his residential condo purchase ... again.

"Hello, Mr. Partner No. 3"—the most anally compulsive person I've ever met in my life. "Yes, I've called the seller's attorney to find out about the changes. Yes. Yes. Yes. Yes, I'll do it right away." I spend 37 minutes drafting a side-letter to the seller's attorney. It's something about an issue the seller and purchaser discussed directly, without informing their attorneys—until now, the eleventh hour.

I hope everything's right in this letter. Partner No. 3 makes me nervous: one of the best in New York City. I run the letter up three flights of stairs while proofing it . . . again. A typo! I turn around, back down the stairs to my office, and revise, print, and proof it. Okay, it's good to go now. Again, I run up the stairs. (We're so lucky to have an internal staircase—otherwise I would never get any exercise besides pushing my pencil.)

After catching my breath, I peak my head into his lavish office, covered with modern art and accolades from a lifetime of achievement. He motions me in to take a seat as he finishes up his conversation with whomever. Seven minutes later, he takes the letter, reads it (pen in hand), makes a few marks, and says it's good to go. He tells me how important it is to get this thing out. It's an emergency.

I take the letter, run back to my office, revise it, and print it *again. Shit!* I forgot to put the letterhead into the printer. Once I place it in manual feed, I run back to my office, click *print* and run back to the printer. No! "Assignment of Leases and Rents"—someone else's document on *my* letterhead! This is a ridiculous waste of time. You would think that, at a big-time New York law firm, we wouldn't have to share printers.

But then, you would think wrong! So I feed the printer again and run through the same drill. Got it this time. Okay. Now I need an overnight slip. I don't have any more, and Linda's not at her desk. Time for another run down that internal staircase.

Down several flights to the mail room, I fetch a whole bunch of slips and envelopes. Then I run back up to my office to fill out the FedEx form and place the letter in the envelope. Done. (Look on the bright side—no need to waste money on a gym membership!)

I've got a pile of yellow fax sheets in my in-box, and reams of comments for another deal I'm working on for yet another partner (Partner No. 4). I'll look at that later. It's 3 p.m. and I *still* haven't gotten to that title and survey. The phone rings again. Partner No. 1. "Yes, I'm working on it. Everything looks good. No, no major issues." Jeez, I certainly *hope* there are no major issues! The truth is, I have no clue yet—I haven't gotten to it. "Yes, I'll bring by my title comments as soon as I'm done. The revisions from last night? There are more changes? Okay. I'll stop by to get them now."

The business people changed the name of the company, so I have to re-revise the documents I revised last night and proofed this morning. What a pain in the ass! The phone rings. Partner No. 3. . . again! What does he want? Maybe I won't answer. I better answer. "Hello, Mr. Partner No. 3. Yes. Yes. Yes, will do." God, help me!

Partner No. 4 drops by with a big grin on his face. "Got plans this weekend?"

"No." A new deal just came in! And there are forty leases that need to be reviewed by Monday. With the most enthusiastic first-year cheer, I accept: "Sure! I'll pitch in. Oh, the other deal? I'm just finishing up those revisions. I'll bring them by as soon as they're done. No problem." What time is it? 4 p.m.—how did that happen? Title and survey, title and survey!

Quick e-mail check. There's something in my in-box from the client to whom I sent the mortgage earlier. What the hell does he want? The mortgage and blackline weren't attached. Damn—what an idiot! My heart now racing, I search the database to find the documents . . . *again*. Finally, I bring them up off the system, create a new e-mail—with the attachments, this time—and re-send. Done.

Alright, where was I? Oh, revisions for Partner No. 1. I'll quickly get them done, do the blacklines, and *then* I'll get to title and survey. I'd better think about ordering dinner—it looks like I'll be here until at least10 p.m And I really have to go to the bathroom—I haven't gone all day.

Back at my desk, I take a two-second breather. Decide what I'm having for dinner. Chinese again. It's easy, fast, and I know exactly what I'll order: One egg roll, Kung Pao Chicken, and a Snapple—it's not glamorous, but it's become the staple of my first year as a big-time corporate attorney.

Alright. I've got to finish these name changes and blacklines for Partner No. 1. He's waiting. As I feverishly work on the revisions, my dinner arrives, but I decide to finish my work before I eat. I'm on a roll, and I really don't have time to eat. It's 7:51. Finally, I'm done with the revisions and leave them on Partner No. 1's chair. It looks like he's gone for the night. He'll have them first thing in the morning. So much for needing them tonight.

The phone rings. It's my mom. "Yeah, I'm still here. No, no I don't know what time I'll be leaving. I'm gonna eat right now. Okay. I gotta go. I'll talk to you tomorrow. Bye." Title and survey. Title and survey.

Oh, *shit!* I completely forgot about my dinner plans tonight. My friends are going to kill me. I make a quick call to one of them. Thank God—voicemail. After leaving an overly apologetic message explaining that I can't make it, I take fifteen minutes to wash down my deliciously cold dinner and finally start what I've been meaning to get to all day long: the title and survey. Now I can finally do something with substance.

I'm tired, though, and my brain isn't working. I'll be here for at least three more hours. That secretarial work really took everything out of me. Is this really what being a corporate lawyer is about? I mean, am I really just a glorified secretary? (And not so glorified, it seems.)

Oh, I just remembered: I still have to record my hours for the last three weeks. *Shit!* I'll do that first thing tomorrow morning...

CHAPTER TWO

THE NATURE OF THE WORK

To sit in darkness here
Hatching vain empires.
—John Milton, Paradise Lost (1667)
Book 2, 1.377

Secretarial Work—Just Part of the Job

As a first-year associate in a large firm, unfortunately, much of the work you will do will entail far too much secretarial work. In addition, you will have little real responsibility and will play a minor role on complex projects.[3] By contrast, working for a small firm or going into your own practice would enable you to work on a variety of smaller projects that would give you a relatively high level of responsibility right from the start.

Paper Clips, Commas, and Empty Spaces

Paper Clips

I was working on a multi-million-dollar deal ($275 million, to be exact) throughout the wee hours of the night—night after night, week after week, including Sundays. When we were ready to close the deal, we needed to make six copies of every single document in the deal (as usual). In other words, we were going to have hundreds of printed pages, all clipped together by paper clips—staples are not used for final documents.[4] Three days before closing, I was visited by the senior associate who was running the deal. I noticed that his skin had turned pasty white, making him look as sickly as I. He walked resolutely into my office, sat down, and made it a point that I should use *large* paper clips. If I were to use small ones, he said he would kill me. He did not laugh. He was not joking. I remember thinking, *Does he think I'm an idiot? I mean, really—look at my $200,000 diplomas! I know enough to use large paper clips; and I've been doing this for three years!* I was pretty insulted. However, now that my head is on straight, what I should have thought, or even said, was: *Are you out of your mind? Large paper clips? Isn't there anything else more important to think about? Is this really what keeps you awake at night?*

Commas

Susan, a dear friend of mine, revised a document for one of the partners in one of the largest law firms in New York, and she failed to insert a comma. Susan made three mistakes: (i) missing the comma, (ii) recycling the original mark-up (i.e.

your comments to the document), and (iii) not attaching it to the revision (something you learned to do in elementary school, remember?). The partner immediately noticed the omission of the comma and informed her about the vital mistake. Susan staunchly defended herself—a common behavior among associates—telling him that he had not inserted a comma where he thought he had inserted it. Unfortunately, she did not have the original mark-up to plead her case, and neither did he. So he made her dig through reams of recycled paper to prove his point (and, I suppose, to humiliate her). It turns out he was right, she had not inserted the comma to reflect his handwritten mark-up.

Empty Spaces

After pulling three all-nighters in a row, I finally printed out multiple documents for a closing. What a relief. It was almost over. But the partner took a quick glance at the final documents before they went into their precisely marked folders for signing. He found an extra space between words. One space! I had to revise the documents *again*.

The Work

Have you ever seen those prospectuses for annual reports and IPOs? Well, someone—some *lawyer*—has spent hundreds of hours drafting and re-drafting each of those documents. What a shame. I mean, who actually reads those things, anyway?

With all the reality shows that fill our TV-watching hours, it's interesting that none of them has to do with litigators, real estate lawyers or corporate lawyers. But then again, who wants to watch someone sitting in an office for two hours shuffling papers around? In fact, the average attorney goes through 20,000 to 100,000 sheets of paper every year, resulting in the release of 4.5 tons of carbon dioxide and other greenhouse emissions.[5] Lawyers use so much paper because of the innumerable revisions that are necessary to write that perfect memo, brief or motion, or to bring a deal from start to finish.

Much of your time as a first- and second-year lawyer at a big firm will be spent on mundane tasks, such as reading tons of e-mails, sending faxes, making copies, scheduling, researching an insignificant portion of an overall litigation and—when you're really lucky—handling some small part of a deal. More often than not, you will not have a clue of how everything fits in to the overall picture, because partners and senior associates have too many other concerns to explain anything to you. You're on your own.

From a logistical standpoint, you will be given a project that will entail writing briefs or reading through documents to "mark them up." Once your work has been performed, you will send them to the other parties working on the transaction and wait for their responses. You will go through several rounds of motions and re-drafts before a deal closes or settlement is reached, or (less frequently) a trial occurs. An associate's work is the most tedious and detail-oriented paperwork that exists within the two basic areas of legal practice in a major firm: litigation and transactional.

Litigation

Litigation is as exciting as it gets when you're in the middle of the OJ trial—a criminal case, mind you. This sort of case does not exist at a large law firm and therefore, work as a litigator at a law firm will never be as fascinating. Occasionally, litigation can be interesting, but the truth be told, 99% of the time, litigation at a big firm is little more than tedious.

Junior litigators prepare their cases by conducting (i) document reviews, which entail sitting in a conference room with other associates, sifting through thousands of pages of documentation looking for evidence to support their cases; (ii) interrogatories, which again involve sitting in a conference room, after having formulated questions on paper, for the interrogation of deponents; (iii) research, which involves sitting in an office in front of the computer with some trips to the library for a diversion, and writing various memos and briefs to give to partners about particular legal questions that arise; and (iv) motion practice, which involves drafting and sending out correspondence to opposing counsel and to the courts about various requirements, requests and deadlines—a logistical nightmare!

The amount of time that goes into preparing for a trial is enormous, especially when it comes to preparing for commercial litigation (e.g., suing Pepsi for copyright infringement)—which most people will end up doing in a law firm. You will spend hours upon hours as a junior associate doing document reviews and writing up endless research about every possible issue. It is highly likely that you will spend a year, two or even more performing these kinds of tasks on one single case alone. And to see the inside of a courtroom at this point, you'd probably have to commit a crime! Most of these cases get settled out of court after years of blood, sweat and tears—and after you've spent a good part of your legal career behind closed doors with nothing more than a computer, a telephone and take-out Chinese.

Realistically, unless you are in your own practice or work for a small firm comprising fewer than twenty lawyers, you will not see the inside of a courtroom as a law firm attorney. There is the occasion when you might visit a courtroom for various motions or for pro-bono cases on which you might work, but more often than not, getting into the courtroom doesn't happen until you are a mid-level or senior associate—after you've earned it. Understandable. Why would any law firm send an inexperienced first-year lawyer into a courtroom? Of course, they *may* send you in as a mute sidekick to bill those hours to the PepsiCos of the world—but that's the most you can expect to do there.

If you prefer immediate gratification, then, and you don't enjoy research and writing, litigation is not for you. But perhaps a little transactional law might do the trick.

Transactional

Unlike litigators, transactional lawyers close deals with a target closing date. The closing date, however, is a *moving* target. Most of the time, it moves away (though occasionally it may move closer).

Most documents used in transactions are form documents with standard legal language that only needs to be revised to reflect the specific terms of each transaction. One basic component in transactional law involves the name of the company (or companies) entering into the deal. The names are inserted on the first and last pages of the document, and it is the name at the end of the document—the almighty signature block—that could cost you your job if you do not get it right. You will spend your first year as a lawyer obsessing over the following signature block:

XYZ Corporation

By:_____
    Name:
    Title:

And you will spend the last years as a lawyer, unless you are a rainmaker (further explored in the next chapter) obsessing over many things, still including the almighty signature block. From the time you begin to churn out the documents, and on to the end of the deal, rest assured: You and your documents will go through at least ten revisions, maybe more. But what could possibly change so many times before the deal closes?

For one, your mistakes alone will occasion many of these revisions. Then, after you've dealt with cleaning up your own mess, you will correct others' mistakes. Mistakes are what you look for as a transactional lawyer—especially as a junior associate. Finding them and correcting them are what you will get paid for. What else takes time?

Deal terms change, dates change, and last, but not least, the name of the company entering the deal changes; therefore, the name for the signature block changes. The documents are negotiated down to the last minute of closing a deal. The partners, the senior associates, and the star mid-levels are the only ones who really know what's going on. They are privy to the negotiations and business issues that determine whether a deal will close on time. As a junior associate, you will be called to make various revisions at any time (2 p.m., 3 p.m., 5 p.m.,

7 p.m., 10 p.m., 2 a.m., and so on around the clock). Most of the changes will have occurred on conference calls for which you were not present. As a junior associate, you will be on your own—always in the dark (sometimes, quite literally).

CHAPTER THREE

POWER AND POLITICS

So industrious bees do hourly strive
To bring their loads of honey to the hives;
Their sordid owners always reap the gains,
And poorly recompense their toils and pains.
—Mary Collier, The Women's Labour (1739)

Ahhh, to Be a Rainmaker

Within the firm, there is a set hierarchy. The *rainmakers*—
the partners who bring in the business and who own equity
stakes (ownership rights and compensation, including pay
through profits) in the firm—are at the top. They are the "big
picture" guys who do not concern themselves with tedium;
they are focused on making the big bucks. Then there are
service partners, who are basically associates for life; they have
titles and they live to service the rainmakers. They either have
equity stakes or non-equity stakes with limited voting rights
and limited compensation. Next are the *associates*, who service
the rainmakers as well and, to a much lesser extent, the service
partners. In between service partners and senior associates are
of counsel lawyers, who more or less function as service partners.

These tiers have subsets, as well, made up of senior and junior levels. For instance, there are *senior* and *junior partners* and *senior* and *junior associates*.

As you might guess, the biggest rainmakers have the most power and the most help, even among the partners themselves. They have the best associates, the best secretaries, and the best paralegals. The service partners have the least experienced associates, secretaries, and paralegals. Frequently, they must fight for assistance with their work; and unfortunately, they are forced to do most of their own work. To a certain extent, the reality is that they are still treated as if they were first-year associates in terms of having to do their own work—*along with* the work of the rainmakers; hence, the title: service partner.

These firms have many committees that keep them running. The rainmakers, who have all of the power, along with service partners, attempt to create cohesive firm policies. And, as anyone knows, to get two people to agree on anything is virtually impossible. Imagine a firm with more than fifty partners? This does not create a very congenial atmosphere for a partnership! These firms are like huge dysfunctional families. And it is no wonder there is such poor management—a topic that is more fully explored in the next chapter.

Junior and Senior Associates

As an associate, the lack of assistance and power is magnified. Junior associates, those associates with three years' experience or less, basically do *everything* for themselves. (Mid-level associates—i.e., those with three to seven years experience—shall be considered junior associates for the purpose of this discussion.) Senior associates, those associates with seven or more years' experience, do *almost* everything for themselves. The difference is that senior associates have more secretarial help and more paralegal help than junior associates, and occasionally a senior associate will engage a junior associate on a deal.

The truth is that junior associates simply do not have enough experience to add any real value. The senior associates, and the service partners for that matter, must definitively know that the work performed below them by junior associates is done correctly. More often than not, it is just easier to do the work themselves than it is to risk having to correct a junior associate's mistakes—amounting to more work in the end.

Senior associates are under a tremendous amount of stress. They must attempt to catch everything, letting nothing slip through the cracks—a difficult task! But when a deal is closing, and there are a million different issues, and the phone won't stop ringing, and the rainmaker needs something else done for a different deal, mistakes will be made.

And beneath all the mayhem lies the biggest worry of all: *What if I fuck up?* This anxiety is prevalent among all attorneys at every level, and the worry only gets worse as you advance in your career. The stress of working on, checking, and re-checking the minute details of the documents never lets up unless you become a rainmaker. Rainmakers don't have to worry about checking and re-checking documents. Of course, being a rainmaker comes with its own set of (even bigger) worries and concerns though.

I would wake up with nightmares about what I might have missed in a document and would dread going to work the next day, thinking: *"Is today the day I will be called in for dropping the ball?"* Simply put, attorneys are put on too many transactions at one time, and the fast pace and urgency to close deals and meet deadlines is unrealistic for any human being. Against this backdrop, it becomes very easy to overlook something. In fact, it is inevitable that *something* will be missed.

The tedious task of review and revision, not to mention anxiety, never changes for service partners and associates. Associates and service partners are on their own; the word *help* really doesn't exist for them.

Support Staff

As a mid-level associate, during an insane period of time, I was assigned ten new deals in ten days. I needed to get a fax out immediately. As I handed over my fax to the head of the fax department, she said to me, "I've got a bone to pick with you. I don't send out faxes with staples. It's not my job to take out staples." I couldn't believe it. I had to deal with this crap from the support staff too, as if crap from the partners, senior associates and clients wasn't enough! This is the respect I get as a fifth-year associate? I didn't take it personally, though, because I've seen support staff speak this way to attorneys with fifteen years' experience. It's sad, but true.

Comments like this from staff abound and are directed mostly at associates. The truth is that they know who's paying the bills. They know who has the power. In addition, they realize that assisting junior associates somehow is not within their job description. The staff will still be there long after associates leave.

Condoning this behavior is a reflection of poor management. And sadly, poor management results in attorneys having to work harder and bill more hours to clients. Of course, more billable hours are extremely beneficial to a firm's bottom line. As a result, there is not much incentive to change the management style, or lack thereof.

CHAPTER FOUR

MANAGEMENT AND THE "NO LIFE" FIRM: BILLABLE AND NON-BILLABLE HOURS

Time hath, my lord, a wallet on his back
Wherein he puts alms for oblivion,
A great-sized monster of ingratitudes:
Those scraps are good deeds past; which are devoured
As fast as they are made, forgot
As soon as done.
—William Shakespeare, *Troilus and Cressida*, 1602, Act 3,
Sc. 3, 1.14

Inefficiencies and Big Profits

Monica was finished for the day, her work completed at 6:00 p.m. It was Thursday, and she was done early, for once. As Monica savored her freedom for the evening, a partner stopped by her office and told her that he needed a round of documents revised before the night was out.

Being the obedient soldier that she was, Monica couldn't refuse his request. She stayed until 1:00 a.m.. Exhausted and sick, she didn't make it to work on Friday. After all, she didn't have anything requiring urgency—for once. And if an emergency were to come up, the partners could always victimize some other associate. Besides, she would have made it to work if that partner hadn't insisted on getting the work done the night before.

As you can see, Monica put in another seven hours—another full day's work—that Thursday night. She easily could have performed the work on Friday morning, when she was refreshed after a decent night's sleep. Most likely, she would have completed her work in four hours instead of seven. Why do partners continually mismanage time . . . and associates?

There is one major goal of firms in connection with the employer–employee relationship: *to record high billable hours*. Believe it or not, poor management contributes to achieving this goal effectively. The lack of good management increases inefficiencies, which, in turn, increase billables and profitability. In effect, good management skills, indispensable to running any other type of successful business, are unnecessary to running a law firm. In fact, good management is a threat to a firm's income. As a consequence, there is really no incentive for the partners to be good managers. It is important to note, however, that clients will dispute bills occasionally; but having the highest possible billables on a transaction or litigation matter will ensure that a firm will get paid the highest possible amount by pushing the envelope, despite a reduction on an invoice.

Beyond record profits to be gained from poor management, lawyers apparently just don't have the skills to be managers. One top law firm instituted a partner mini-course in etiquette.[6] The slide presentation included bullet points on how to treat associates. For example, say, "Thank you" and "Good work"; "Return associates' phone calls as quickly as you would a partner's or client's"; "Be sensitive to not canceling associates' vacations"; "Refrain from subjecting associates to profanity-laced tirades in which you tell them they should be fired"; and "Don't tell gay associates that they like taking it up the ass (because they might be tops rather than bottoms)."[7]

For the most part, lawyers were students first—not business people, not managers. They have been trained to think, do research, and write. Managing people is not a part of the course load at law school, although it should be. In addition, whereas most business people have worked a number of years before attending graduate school, most lawyers attend law school right out of college, so they have no real-life experience. The lawyers who start their careers in a law firm and end up making partner inevitably perpetuate the operations of a law firm because it's the only thing they've ever known. I would venture to say that most associates who make partner were those who went straight from college to law school and on to a law firm. This makes the lack of management endemic to law-firm culture and consequently, ensures high billable hours.

When the thirty-year old lawyer died, he said to St. Peter, "How can you do this to me?—A heart attack at my age? I'm only thirty." Replied St. Peter: "When we looked at your total hours billed we figured you were ninety-five."

—Anonymous

Achieving Billable Hours

Another aspect of law firm life that is incurable is the billable hour. *Keeping time* is the most important aspect of law firm life. Every single minute must be billed. It is advisable and expected that you bill *everything*—even if you run to the bathroom or take a fifteen-minute break. An attorney at one of the biggest law firms in the world felt that this billing practice was unethical, and she refused to bill for breaks. Needless to say, that job didn't work out for her.

Having continued high billable hours is ideal for an associate. One lawyer who had been putting in about 2,600 billable hours a year for several years was diagnosed with cancer. (It's worth noting that a total of 2,000 hours a year equals a workday from about 9:00 a.m. to 7:00 p.m., five days a week.) After time off, surviving and returning to work, her hours came in at about 2,300—not too shabby for someone having had cancer! Hell, that's not too shabby for someone who *didn't* have cancer. But what did the firm have to say about this? "Why are your hours so low?"

High billable hours derive from too much work for one individual, coupled with inherent inefficiencies. Junior, midlevel and even senior associates perform tasks that qualified secretaries can do (unbeknownst to clients), in order to reach the highest billable hours. Consider, for instance, the almighty signature block illustrated back in Chapter Two. Countless hours have been spent drafting and re-drafting these signature blocks. What's more, associates (and even partners) spend hours upon hours each year sending faxes. Yes, that's right. As a junior associate, you will be a glorified secretary (and you won't even be that good at it, since it's not what you were trained to do). Of course, there is nothing wrong, in and of itself, with performing these tasks, and everyone should know how to send a fax, in case of an emergency. The problem is that everything is *always* an emergency. As a result, young associates are trying to learn and deal with legal issues and simultaneously performing secretarial tasks. Not to mention that the client is spending thousands of dollars for something a secretary can do. But I guess that's the point.

Why, you might ask, can't the secretary and other support staff just assist with these jobs? Associates must perform these mundane tasks for several reasons, but the primary reason is that the secretaries leave promptly at 5:30 p.m. most of the time, so they are not available to send a fax if you wanted them to. In addition, even if they are physically present, they may be dealing with a more important person (i.e., a partner), so you're stuck doing the mundane work for yourself. Firms do not hire more secretarial and support staff, because this would cut into the profits. Partners would rather have junior associates send faxes because it costs their clients more money. Again, there is nothing wrong with getting the job done. And there is nothing wrong with paying your dues. It only becomes a problem when you realize that you can't get out of work to live your life because of how much time you spend having to send e-mails, faxes, and overnight packages to clients.

Becoming the Billable Hour

Daily Journals

As I ruefully sat in a senior associate's office, I glanced at his bookshelf, where he had deal binders, reference books, and firm pamphlets. He also had, on the very bottom shelf, ten red daily planners lined up neatly. This is where he had kept all of his time for the past ten years of his life. He had every minute of every day recorded in those books. For some, this might be interesting, and even a bit alluring; but for me, it was scary . . . *very, very scary*. I was actually horrified. What was written in those books was not journal entries of introspection or insights into life. It was all monotonous scribbles describing hundreds of conference calls, meetings, and drafting sessions that had taken place over ten long years. In a nutshell, it was what drives a law firm—and what kills lawyers' souls.

There will be innumerable dates and appointments to cancel. Only your lawyer colleagues will understand your last-minute cancellations and phone calls returned three weeks late. All your other friends with "normal" lives just think you are inconsiderate and crazy; they don't understand why you can't just leave.

Why not go home early and deal with the work the next day? The answer is *No—your work is never done, and it can never wait until the next day*. If a brief is due, or a deal is actually closing, there is work to be done until the money hits the wire. Even afterwards, there are the post-closing items. If clients want something, you give it to them *now*. There is no waiting, and there is no saying, "I'm unable to get to it right now." The answer "No" is unacceptable, which results in always feeling that you're behind and can never catch up to the present moment. In law firms, *now* is the prime directive for everything. But the fact is that it is humanly impossible to get to everything *now*.

To sum it up, as an associate, your clients are the partners, and the partners simply don't give a shit about your personal life. They own you. They will tell the client that it will get done and will leave to go to a concert with the very same client while you are in the office drafting, e-mailing and faxing the documents that the client doesn't even need until a week later, after she gets back from vacation. Of course, the partner doesn't tell you this, so you are unable to manage your workload—or your life—efficiently. If there were just the slightest communication among partners, senior associates, and junior associates, everyone would be able to manage their time a bit better.

There will be all-nighters reminiscent of your old college days; the difference is that, afterwards, you still have to go to work the next day . . . and the day after that. No sleeping in after your 9:00 a.m. exam. It's back to the office after a quick run home to take a shower. If you're lucky enough, you'll be working for a firm that has its own showers, and you'll never have a reason to go outside.

In addition to spending hours actually doing your work, you must spend more hours entering your billable time. Lucky for you, the technology is user-friendly, so you will be able to enter your summaries for yourself as a junior associate, which is a good thing—because the secretaries will be too busy to help you anyway. All your time spent must be recorded. These are the hours for which the clients pay—entries much like the following:

Transactional:

> *Client Matter 656/333:*
> *Review and revision of lease; Conference Call with client re: issues; Draft comment letter re: lease.*

> *Client Matter 678/986:*
> *Draft Mortgage and ancillary documents; meeting with partner re: same; c/c with title company re: same.*

Litigation:

> *Client Matter 009/042:*
> *Research re: venue; draft memo re: same; draft motion letters and correspondence.*

And so on . . .

Notice that these time entries do not disclose faxing and the more secretarial duties . . . for obvious reasons. On average, for all firm sizes, total hours worked are 2,068, with 1,838 hours billed.[8] As firm size increases, the total number of hours worked increases.[9] The average billable hours required for all law firm sizes are 1,888.[10] In addition, most firms (77.4%) treat pro bono work as the equivalent of a billable hour, with approximately half capping this category at fifty hours.[11] Beyond billable hours, most firms also require non-billable hours.

Non-Billable Hours

Yes, you must log your non-billable time to show your commitment to the firm, as if doing all-nighters countless times a year isn't enough. This will include department meetings, seminars, firm-wide meetings, firm outings, and other events—all in a lame attempt to record every minute of what has become of your life. This time-keeping requirement does not stop once you become a partner. As an attorney, you will always "keep your time," unless you go in-house—i.e., working as an attorney who is an employee of a corporation.

After all your billables and non-billables at the largest firms, you'll end up earning about $61.00 an hour.[12] This doesn't sound all that bad, but you must consider that, if you take any vacation, these billables must fit into a shorter time period. Also bear in mind that the work will not be steady, so you might work ninety hours one week and forty another. And all the hours spent in the office will not be billable either, because no one is that efficient.

Are there any options better than spending an average of 2,000 hours in the office? What about "Life Style" firms, i.e., those firms that promise fewer hours and more time for your own life? Answer: There is no such thing as a "Life Style" firm. In short, what inevitably happens at these firms is that you will receive less pay and end up working just as hard as in a "No Life" firm. And after years of toil and futile attempts to lead a balanced life, you might consider part-time work. Perhaps this is the way to achieve a reprieve.

CHAPTER FIVE

PART-TIME AND CONTRACT WORK

Part Time: Work Less for Less Pay

Finally, I got what I wanted: a part-time job! After years of searching, there was a firm that would give me a chance to work as a part-timer. Sure, I took a pay cut but I only had to work four days a week.

I really believed I had it good working only four days a week. After all, a friend of mine took a part-time job from 9:00–5:30 five days a week. That was her "part-time" deal. As it turns out, I wasn't so lucky. I was fitting five days of work into four and taking work home consistently. The worst part of it was that I was actually getting paid less.

Part-time is a fallacy—and virtually non-existent at a big law firm. The percentage of part-timers in large law firms is 5.9%, and of those, 73% are women.[13] First, it is extremely difficult to work part-time as an attorney, because the industry is service-based. Service-based means *on demand*, and if you are part-time, you are not on demand. The consequence is that law firms shun part-timers. In addition, if you have a goal of becoming a partner, part-time will only delay, if not end, partnership possibilities. In a nutshell, it is a stigmatized status with barriers to advancement.[14] These same firms, however, may all boast about their part-time programs, but what they don't say is that the people to whom they give part-time or "flex-time" more often than not work the same number of hours in fewer days. In other words, five days of work in four, or six days in four-and-a- half; but at least they will let you take the work home! How thoughtful: You can spend your weekend at the beach reviewing legal documents.

So, is there a way to achieve a work–life balance while continuing to work at a firm? The answer is "Yes"—but it does not come without faults of its own.

Contract Work

You can work as a temporary—or contract—attorney and do project-based work that you hear about and, are ultimately hired, through legal employment agencies. There are long-term projects that can last for more than three months to more than two years, and short term projects that can last only one day and as long as three months. Even though there is uncertainty practicing law in this manner (since you never know when a project will come up), you will have time to lead a balanced lifestyle without being a slave to the law.

The down side is that you will be giving up a steady income, benefits, bonuses, and perks. Even worse, it is possible that becoming a temp will typecast you, and you may have a difficult time getting permanent, full-time work again.[15] You are essentially halting your career. And after all that, you still might have to put in long hours. For me, I actually didn't mind working until 1:00 a.m., because I knew it was short-term, and

I was getting paid by the hour. I could give my absolute best, do excellent work and leave without feeling guilty and without the long-term stress that is inherent in being a full-time associate.

As a contract attorney, you will have freedom to get your work done without someone breathing down your neck. You are expected to get the work done without guidance. After all, you will be brought in to work on overflow and ensure that deadlines are met. Independence and minimal interference are great rewards of being a contract attorney. It's like being your own employer at times. You come into work and, most of the time, sit in a windowless office in a little corner away form the permanent employees. You're pretty much hidden from view and, as a result, are able to get your work done quickly and efficiently without distraction. You are on your own, and it is up to you to get the work done correctly. What associates and partners do not want from contract attorneys is work that has errors, or a temp who needs help. The whole point is to bring you in to get work done quickly, efficiently, correctly and without any required work from the top ranks.

One of my best projects lasted two and a half years. Initially, I had my own office with a window and worked about a forty hour week. Since space was tight, my office was located on a different floor and in a different department from where I received my assignments. I worked independently and received my work requests via e-mail. After about six months, I, along with five other temps, was relegated to what was basically a large storage room, which was not half as bad as it sounds. There were empty offices around the perimeter, so for argument sake, we did have a "windowed office." There were other temps placed at various places around the firm as well.

We received work requests via phone or e-mail and rarely saw the attorneys for whom we worked. We had control over our work flow and the hours we put in. For example, partners and associates would send e-mails asking about our availability to work on a project, and we were able to accept or decline the request. We could work on one deal at a time or several, depending on how many hours we wanted to work. There were temps who worked eighty hours a week and others who worked thirty. In addition, after having proved myself, I was able to work from home from time to time, and other temps chose to work from home as well at times. It was actually a very positive experience for me, and I could say that I was satisfied with my career for the first time. The number-one reason for my satisfaction was that I had control over my life for the first time in many years. It must be noted that not all the contract attorneys were satisfied with their work situations, since many actually wanted permanent positions. Nonetheless, on the whole, the structure worked very well for the temps and the firms.

I did not receive, and did not care about, the $65,000 bonus that the first-year associates received along with their $160,000 base salary. I have to admit, for a split second I thought about all the compensation I had given up as a temp, but then a flood of my not so happy existence as an associate in a big firm came washing over me, and I knew I had made the right decision. By the way, I wasn't the only one shocked at these figures. All the other temps were quite surprised as well. Especially since, as it turned out, the mid-level and senior associates and partners were turning to the temps to get the work done instead of using first-years, which is usually the case in the law firm structure. In fact, using the temps had become an issue with the executive committee because the first-years weren't getting work and learning what they should have as junior attorneys.

For firms, getting work done right the first time, without having to correct work or train anyone, is one of the perks of using a contract attorney. What is more, if there are any non-performers, the firms simply tell the agency that they no longer want the services of a particular temp. They do not have to go through the arduous task of firing someone and giving them a severance package. As for the good temps, the firms simply keep them and raise hourly rates periodically and are assured that work is completed not only in a timely fashion, but also correctly and without the bother of having to teach or train anyone.

One irritating aspect about being a contract attorney, however, is that, while partners, mid-levels and senior associates are aware of the value of a temp and realize the point of their presence, junior associates do not. Somehow they seem to think that contract attorneys are beneath them and that it is their turn to tell someone what to do and have them make revisions to their work, which, as discussed earlier, is work for secretaries. So, as a contract attorney, you will most likely have to explain to junior associates your purpose and experience and that you are not a part of the firm hierarchy. What is interesting about this issue is the reason why it exists at all: poor management. Senior and mid-level attorneys should only interact with the contract attorneys or explain to junior associates the role of a temp attorney in order to avoid unnecessary confrontations.

If windows are not that important to you, and you are someone who just likes to come and go as you complete your work, without having to worry about face time, as full-time associates must do, then temping could be a good alternative to full-time employment. In order to make a decent hourly rate, however, it is important that you are employed for at least three years on a permanent basis in a firm to gain the experience needed to land a good project. Otherwise, as a recent graduate without experience, you will be relegated to sorting through thousand of pages of documents and data input on enormous litigation cases.

If uncertainty is not a problem for you, practicing law as a temp can give you a decent paycheck and *freedom*. The best part of temping is that you won't have to deal with office politics; and by landing the right projects, you can make in six months what most people make in a year or more. In addition, your hourly rate will most likely be higher than the hourly rate of full-time attorneys for specialized practice areas. If you've practiced law for five years or more, in any area, you can make a good hourly rate of at least $65.00 and possibly $150 per hour in New York with projects requiring special knowledge.[16] If you are a recent graduate or an attorney at any level, you can perform document review projects in connection with litigation cases for about $35.00-$40.00 per hour in New York.[17]

So, what is the trade-off? What types of benefits and perks will you be giving-up? What do attorneys bring home on an annual basis?

CHAPTER SIX

The Package

Compensation

While you sit in your office and see the clock strike 10:00 p.m. *yet again*, or you're in the office Saturday and Sunday *yet again*, you will tell yourself, *yet again*, that you are getting paid handsomely, and late hours and weekends aren't so bad. And after all, you have nothing better to do with your time anyway, right? When partners scream at you for not inserting a comma or deleting a space, you'll tell yourself, *yet again*, that you're getting paid quite a bit of money. In fact, a partner corroborated this very thing to another one of my fellow attorneys. He told him that he "was getting paid to take it," and that was that. It is interesting to note that 84.2% of mid-level associates would take pay cuts for fewer billable hours.[18] Well, actually, how much do you get paid in exchange for your life?

The average profits per equity partner in America's 100 top-grossing law firms was $1,260,000 in 2009, and sixteen firms reported profits per equity partner of more than $2,000,000, virtually unchanged from 2008.[19] Equity partners take home most of the big bucks, whereas non-equity partners make less than half their equity cohorts,[20] And making equity partner has become increasingly difficult.[21] It takes about ten years to make partner, and there is no guarantee that you'll ever get there. Actually, the odds of making equity partner are very low—dismal at best, especially at the largest firms.[22]

As a point of interest and in stark contrast to compensation for entry-level attorneys working in non-firm positions, such as public defenders (whose median salary was $47,000) and state and local prosecutors (whose median staring salaries were $50,000 and $45,675, respectively),[23] the median starting compensation for first-year associates in law firms with more than 251 attorneys was $145,000 nationwide, and those with more than 251 attorneys in major cities (New York, Boston, Chicago, Los Angeles, San Francisco Bay, the Silicon Valley area, and Washington, D.C.) was $160,000.[24] The median starting salary for firms of all sizes was $120,000 in 2008.[25] In addition, law firms vary with the size of their salary increases each successive year, but generally the increases are between $10,000 and $25,000 per year, based on billable criteria.[26] The criteria appear to be objective, but once inside a law firm, you will find that these "objective" standards have a very discretionary element, which may result in a reduction of the salary increase, or even in no increase at all.

It is important to note that firms will not compensate you for working more than a part-time schedule if you are a part-time employee, and chances are that you will never recoup your losses for putting in long hours to get your work done.

Bonuses

Sarah, a former colleague of mine, billed the required number of hours to qualify for the year-end bonus and was looking forward to the extra $15,000. She spent 200 hours researching and writing an article for one of the partners, who told her these hours would count toward her billable hours. Well, it turned out that they did *not* count, and Sarah did not get her bonus. If she had only known, she wouldn't have volunteered her time to writing this article.

Bonuses are generally given on the basis of an objective billable standard, along with subjective factors and experience.[27] Bonuses are typically $10,000 to $25,000.[28] In 2006, bonuses topped out at $65,000 at the largest firms.[29] In 2007, some firms paid out as much as $110,00 for their most senior associates.[30] What law firms will not disclose is that billables may be reduced and that non-billables, though a requirement of law firm life, do not count towards bonuses. And even if there is a promise that certain non-billables will count towards bonuses (e.g., writing articles for publication on behalf of partners), chances are that the promise can be broken—as we saw in Sarah's case.

Of course, if you are a "star-associate" (which typically means giving your life away and not questioning anything), you are likely to be compensated. One of my colleagues, Ken, was a star associate. He needed twenty more billable hours to make his bonus. He billed twenty hours towards putting deal binders together—a task that usually takes no more than one or two hours for an associate. The partner on the deal, who was also the head of the department, saw Ken's hours on the preliminary bill (a bill that clients don't see—they only receive a final one-page invoice) and said, "Twenty hours for binders?" That was the extent of the partner's reprimand, if one can even call it that. Ken got his bonus. Most associates are not "stars," and non-star associates will not get this type of leniency; they end up getting these padded hours shaved off their billable requirements.

Benefits

You will most likely receive a certain amount of health coverage, life insurance (which is calculated on the basis of a certain percentage of your salary), disability insurance, and a 401k. These benefits are acceptable, except for the 401k.

Unlike most companies, generating millions of dollars in revenue, in most firms there is no such thing as matching (or even partial) contributions. Unfortunately, lawyers are not typically business people, and they frequently do not even ask 401k benefit questions before accepting their offers. But it wouldn't matter anyway, because firms will almost never contribute. It is an unwritten rule—and typically a non-negotiable. The only money that goes into the 401k is yours. With the amount of profits the law firms generate, you will undoubtedly find yourself thinking that they should. Over the years, a firm's contribution can add up to be hundreds of thousands of dollars. And after spending your life in your office night after night, year after year, contributing to big firm profits, this is something you will begin to resent.

Perks

In New York, if you work until after 8:00 p.m., you might receive up to $25.00 for dinner and a car home. On weekends, you might be allotted a total of $45.00 for all meals throughout the day and a car to and from the office. Eventually, you might be offered baseball tickets—probably only after you've been with the firm for five or more years (a perk that's hardly worth the wait). In any event, you probably won't have time to go anyway.

Vacation

Firms usually give about four weeks' vacation a year and have a "use it or lose it policy." Most lawyers do not have the time to take their vacations, so they end up losing them. When attorneys do schedule vacations, or actually go on them, many times they must be cancelled, cut short, or rescheduled. Vacations are usually scheduled for one-week intervals because firms don't like associates to be away from the firm for more than one week at a time.

Rest assured that, as an associate, you will be working double time before you leave and after you get back, and you will probably be expected to be on call during your vacation. Everyone is too busy with their own work to cover for you when you are gone. Sure, a colleague might take a few phone calls but will certainly not take on any of your work. They want time to breathe themselves. And who can blame them?

A friend of mine once said to me, "If a bartender were to go on vacation, he or she wouldn't have to make up for all those drinks he or she didn't make during vacation." But as a lawyer, there can be no gap in time or work. The clock is always ticking, and your work is always waiting for you. Attorneys often say that it is actually easier not to go on vacation because of the increased daily hours required beforehand and afterwards.

The overall compensation package at first seems to be wonderful, and perhaps it actually is. But nothing is for free. For the salary and benefits and sometime bonuses, the firms have first dibs on your time at any time.

You might think the money and decent lifestyle will make up for the fact that you spend all of your time working and paying your dues. It seems only logical. But in time, the money can't compensate for lost time and for work that is far less satisfying than you thought it would be. The attrition rate alone (seventy-eight percent for attorneys who have worked for their firms for approximately five years) is a good indication that money is not enough to keep attorneys in law firms.[31] Besides, if you do not decide to leave of your own volition, the statistics show (as more fully discussed in Chapter Eight) that you will likely be told that you will not be making partner. In other words, you will be asked to leave.

CHAPTER SEVEN

WOMEN AND MINORITIES

*Women have one great advantage over men. It is commonly
thought that if they marry they have done enough, and need a career
no further. If a man marries, on the other hand, public opinion is all
against him if he takes this view.*

—Rose Macaulay

Minority women make up just 1.88% of partners, and
minority men account for 4.17%.[32] Overall, minorities make
up 19.08% of associates and 6.05% of partners, and minority women account for 10.73% of associates.[33] In law school,
women make up 46.7% of enrollment.[34] Nationally, the total
number of female associates is 45.66%.[35] By their seventh year,
88% of women have left their firms, as compared with 63% of
their male counterparts.[36] By the time partnership arrives, if at
all (about ten years later), women make up a mere 19.21% of
partners.[37] Where did these women go, and why?

Fifty percent of women who leave firms continue to work
either in the law as in-house counsel or in the nonprofit sector,
and 46% leave the practice of law altogether.[38] The primary
reason for leaving is "difficulty integrating work and family/
personal life" (more than 60%).[39] Other commonly cited

reasons for leaving (in descending order of prevalence) are "long work hours" (just under 62%), "workload pressures" (54%), "poor promotion opportunities" (40%), and an "unsupportive work environment" (32%).[40]

The women who do decide to stick with practicing law in firms appear to give up marriage and children. In fact, 39% of women in firms were never married, as compared to 29% in the same age group (27–32) in the general population, and the percentage of women attorneys without children in that age group is as high as 76%, whereas only 36% of the women in the general population have had no children.[41] On the flip side, more male attorneys are likely to be married than men in the general population in the same age group than female attorneys.[42]

Many women must choose between a successful career and a family, and some women simply make compromises between their family and work life. One attorney is very happy working full-time, but she knows that the only reason she can "do both" is that she has a full-time nanny, whereas other women just choose to leave the workplace.[43] One judge stated that she is not so sure she would be on the bench if she were married with children.[44]

The women who do choose to work in law firms have many battles to fight. Other than having to fit into the male-dominant firm culture, they have to fight for their work. Men generally get "the good work," and getting better work, or more valuable work, ultimately leads to better pay.

The pay gap between men and women increasingly widens on the path to partnership. For instance, on average, women earn $7,000 less than men in annual pay as associates, $14,000 less as of-counsel, $23,000 less as non-equity partners, and $87,000 less as equity partners, with the average compensation for a male equity partner equaling $660,000, while the average for a female is $573,000.[45] Greater pay for more valuable work only stands to reason, but the question is: Why do the men get the better work?

One simple reason could be the high attrition rate among women, the assumption being that "She will eventually leave, so we won't give her so much responsibility." Another, more likely, reason is the male-dominated culture that prevails in most firms.

Men vs. Women in Workplace Culture

Jack and Joe

One of my colleagues, Jack, took one month off to study for the bar exam (he had already taken and passed the Florida bar and needed to take the New York bar since he had decided to relocate to New York). During this month, I had daily contact with Joe, the partner for whom Jack usually worked. Prior to Jack's temporary departure, I would rarely even talk to Joe. For me, this was a nice change of pace, working hand in hand with a partner. We got along well—or so I thought. I had all the answers, or at least found all the answers, for Joe when he asked. I gave him deal updates on a regular basis. But when Jack came back, I hardly had any more contact with Joe. In fact, he took the deal on which I had been working away from me and gave it to Jack to finish. Joe didn't even have the courtesy to tell me this; Jack just waltzed into my office and said, "Joe wants me to work on this deal." I asked Jack why, and he said he didn't know. I was an idiot for asking the question; I (as well as everyone else in the department) knew that Jack was Joe's favorite.

Jack looked like Joe; he even had the same mannerisms. In fact, one day I walked past Joe's office, and he and Jack were both happily picking their noses in tandem. How could I compete with that?

One former colleague of mine who practiced at a top-five law firm for ten years was told, when they "let her go," that "she was not, nor ever would be, a part of the boys' club." But they got good use out of her for all those years, and it is apparent that she was quite a good lawyer, because the firm never would have kept her for that long if she hadn't been. The truth is that there were never any women partners in the real estate practice area of Usem & Losem, and, sadly, they were not about to start with her.

That is not to say that partnership for women is impossible. After all, 19.21% of women in firms are partners. But as a woman, you have to prove yourself to show that you are in it for the long run in order to get career- and compensation-advancing work. You have to show that you want to work and are interested in being a key player, and you must get involved outside the office, take on pro bono work, be willing to write articles and agree to be on call at all times.[46] According to Bittina B. Plevin, a top-rated partner at Proskauer Rose LLP, "You have to say 'I want.'"[47] In essence, you have got to be committed and aggressive. The caveat is that you may very well prove yourself along the way, but it is no guarantee of partnership. As is common knowledge, it is extremely difficult to make partner. The chances are slim at best.

CHAPTER EIGHT

Money can't buy happiness.
—Mid-19th-Century Proverb

Overall, for firms (including those with two or more attorneys), the annual attrition rate is 19%.[48] By the fifth year of employment, the attrition rate at law firms is staggering. The attrition rate of all attorneys leaving their first jobs out of law school, inclusive of firms with two or more associates, was almost 80%, with 40% leaving within three years of their start dates.[49] For lateral hires (i.e., those hired from other firms), for the class of 1998, of 251–500 attorneys, 52.3% left their firms within the first three years of employment.[50] Interestingly, in firms with 100 or fewer lawyers, 69% of attorneys left by the fifth year of employment.[51] The fact that there is such a high attrition rate among smaller firms suggests that these firms have cultures similar to those of their larger counterparts. The big question is "Why is there such a high attrition rate—why are attorneys leaving their firms in droves?"

Sixty percent of those who leave their firms stated long work hours, and over 50% sated work-load pressures as the primary reasons for leaving.[52] Other reasons for leaving were inflexible work hours (20% for men, and 30% for women) and the difficulty in achieving a work-life balance (40% for men, and 60% for women).[53] In addition, 30% of attorneys left their firms due to an unsupportive work environment.[54] Only 10% stated leaving for better compensation.[55] Other than these very specific reasons for leaving their firms, what lies beneath is the tried and true reason for lawyers jumping ship: general unhappiness. The caveat is that research has failed to demonstrate that these law firm lawyers are generally dissatisfied with their career choice. In fact, national surveys reveal and acknowledge contradictory evidence of the opposite sentiment: satisfaction.

As would be expected, solo practitioners and associates in smaller firms, as well as attorneys working in government and public interest positions, report the highest level of job satisfaction inclusive of the work setting itself, the substance of the work, and the social value of the work, but excluding compensation.[56] In fact, the larger the firm is, the lower the expressions of career satisfaction, with satisfaction decreasing as firm size increases.[57]

Higher levels of satisfaction at small firms can be attributed to many factors. As would be expected, the atmosphere at small firms is less formal and more collegial. Lawyers have high levels of responsibility early in their careers and are able to work on a broad range of projects. In addition, working in a small firm enables attorneys to get noticed more easily and attain partnership in a shorter period of time.

My brother-in-law made partner just after five years of practice and is the happiest, most satisfied attorney I have met in my life. He not only made partner after five years but also didn't have to kill himself to make partner. He had tons of client contact and even went to trial several times during those first five years. Lastly, he made it home for dinner every night (not to mention an early-afternoon margarita or two on many occasion) and never had to cancel any vacation plans.

On the flip side, the practice of law in large firms is formal and competitive, the work can be mundane and highly specialized, the hours are grueling and partnership, for the most part, is a pipe dream. The difficult and challenging environment in which these lawyers work partially explains the high attrition rates within the first five years of working at these firms.

Even though 80% of lawyers report satisfaction with their decision to become a lawyer,[58] the most important reason in determining whether to leave their firm or organization would be general job dissatisfaction.[59] It would seem to follow, then, that the high turnover rate at firms is due to lawyer dissatisfaction.

Why the contradiction in sentiment? First and foremost, the issue of lawyers' satisfaction with practicing law has been the subject of a plethora of research over the past twenty-five years and has proven to be a complex, multi-layered question. Questions relating to job setting, social good, work hours, work environment and compensation result in different answers, as would be expected. Lawyers are human beings (believe it or not) and can very easily be satisfied with one aspect of practicing law (i.e., compensation but—ironically—not enough for firms to retain them) and extremely dissatisfied with another (i.e., the grueling work hours). In any case, the tons of sponsored research, the numerous articles and the blogs relating to lawyers' dissatisfaction and unhappiness with the practice of law are enough proof that a problem exists.

Perhaps the studies and surveys do not ask the right questions (e.g., "Would lawyers choose the same path if they had it to do all over again?" "Do they enjoy what they do on a daily basis?" "Do they love what they do?" "Is it bearable?" Or "Is it unbearable?"). Perhaps it is a lawyer's ability to break things down and compartmentalize things quite easily. For instance, to ask about whether lawyers are satisfied with their career decision is so general that, instead of focusing on the negative, daily grind, they focus on the satisfying, positive aspects of their career choice, such as the education, prestige, social good and compensation. Perhaps lawyers really secretly are satisfied with their career choice (difficult to believe) and just lie about it under peer pressure, since countless lawyers in conversation say that they do not like what they do. Yet another possibility, based on a more plausible psychological tenet, is cognitive dissonance. Lawyers who have just spent tens of thousands of dollars on their educations (excluding the cost of their undergraduate studies) are not so willing to admit defeat and say that they are not satisfied with their career decision. In any case, there are many reasons lawyers can concoct in order to say they are satisfied; but again, the available literature on the subject, as well as the indirect evidence to the contrary, is astonishing.

Advertisements, publications, and course offerings are indicative of lawyers' dissatisfaction with their careers. For instance, in *The New York Times* every Sunday, there is a classified job advertisement that reads, "Running from the Law?" I also came across a course offering entitled, "Other Careers for Lawyers." There is an entire 400-page book called, *What Can You Do With a Law Degree?* What is more, dissatisfaction with the practice of law exists beyond the United States. A

Canadian newspaper, the *National Post*, reported the prevalence of unhappy lawyers in an article aptly titled "Legal Exodus."[60]

In addition, the fact that nearly 20% of attorneys in practice from two to twenty years abuse alcohol (compared to 10% of the general population) is likely a testament to their high levels of dissatisfaction and stress, and this percentage increases to 25% for attorneys in practice for more than twenty years.[61] Attorneys also report a higher incidence of depression as compared to non-lawyers similarly situated demographically.[62] Is it no wonder so many attorneys leave their firms?

Attrition can be attributed to attorneys voluntarily leaving their jobs, as one-half to two-thirds of attorneys do so.[63] The others get fired or laid-off. And how do firms go about firing their employees?

Firings

Several years after her layoff, Sarah, the non-star associate mentioned in Chapter Eight, told me that she had just run into one of the partners at our former firm. To her surprise, he actually said to her, "Yeah, we made it through hard times, and we didn't even have to lay anyone off." If even partners are kept in the dark about the axe, certainly the public at large won't find out.

The Facts

Yes, law firms dole out plenty of pink slips, but the world at large, and even the insiders, do not seem to hear about it. Firings are kept on the Q-T because law firms don't want to tarnish their reputations, which tout job security. Announcements will only be made under the most dire circumstances; the Internet bubble burst couldn't hide the effects it had on law firms, nor could the 2008–2009 market spurred by the sub-prime mortgage crisis and corporate malfeasance. During ordinary times— even good times—however, firms conceal the fact that they fire quite a number of associates every year. The lack of reporting should not be taken to mean that working at a law firm will ensure a high level of job security.

Keep in mind that law firms must "let people go" because they hire too many graduates from law school in the first place. As each year passes, there is not the need for as many mid-level associates or senior associates. As a result, firms must fire people because the volitional attrition rate does not resolve a law firm's natural tendency towards top-heaviness. In a large firm, it's up or out.

The Process of Getting Axed and the Tell-Tale Signs: Reviews

So, how do firms go about firing their devout worker bees? Simply put, the partners mark the ones who don't fit in and fire them for cause (i.e., non-performance and incompetence) in a formal review. Once an attorney or group of attorneys have been marked, surely they will know it. They will no longer receive work. If they do, it will be work from the least powerful partners in the firm—the ones who have to do their own work most of the time. These marked attorneys know their time is limited and will just be waiting for the axe to fall.

As the end of their time with the firm approaches, these attorneys will usually face a review that they will probably sense is going to be their last. There will be several reasons cited, no doubt—some quite ludicrous, and others actually degrading. One of my very close friends was fired because she missed a period at the end of a sentence! Perhaps they will be told (in not so many words) that they are imbeciles: "We are letting you go because you show a lack of understanding about overall deal structure and a lack of knowledge and understanding of legal documentation generally." Of course, it is quite hard to believe that people who have graduated from top law schools or at the top of their class at other law schools do not understand what is going on. Or maybe they will be told that "We do not see that you are committed to the firm"—this after working weekends and pulling all-nighters for months on end. Unfortunately, however, in firms presumably dedicated to the pursuit of justice, justice does not always prevail.

In general, law firms do not want to admit to layoffs. If law firms were to publicize layoffs, they would be showing weakness.[64] Even during the recession of 2008–2009, firms adhered to the inhumane way in which they fired people. Attorneys were still let go based on negative performance reviews, even though everyone knew that it was the economy that forced people out.[65] This is not to say that there aren't incompetent attorneys working in law firms. Certainly there are—but not as many as the performance reviews would suggest, and not as many as the firings that take place because of a lack of space at the top. Granted, it is most likely that the attorneys laid off were not the top performers. But just because attorneys are not at the top of the performance scale does not mean that their performance is substandard, as most firms would have you believe. Even if the firings are not always fair, and the performance reviews on which they are based are nothing more than a smokescreen, lawyers who get the axe do find out that there is a bright side to getting fired.

Severance Packages: A Glimmer of Light

What law firms do excel at is the severance packages they dole out like candy. Most firms give two months' salary, benefits, and career counseling after firing you. What is more, during the two months of getting full pay plus benefits, you can usually utilize your office, computer, and other equipment to facilitate your job search. You won't be expected to perform any work, since, for all intents and purposes, you no longer exist.

The primary reason for being so generous is that firms do not want to get bad publicity. They have enough trouble retaining employees in the first place. In fact, reputation is of such importance that one top firm during the 2008–2009 recession, White & Case LLP, paid its first-year lawyers $45,000 *not* to work, and $75,000 to those who "volunteer."[66] In light of the economic bloodshed, which is more than a good reason to rescind offers and not pay at all, this firm did the right thing . . . the ethical thing. Ironically, firms tend to come through when they fire you, and it doesn't matter if they do it just to sweeten the sour grapes and avoid lawsuits. The result is the same: They do it, and attorneys have a bit of time to figure out what to do next.

What's Next on the Agenda?

What do these lawyers do when they leave? Many go (i) to other firms, (ii) into their own practices, (iii) in-house, (iv) into public service jobs, or (v) to undertake family responsibilities.[67] In addition, others leave to return to school, pursue other careers and job opportunities or travel to see the world and finally figure out what they want to do with their lives.

On the bright side, it is important to note that lawyers who have moved out of big firms to in-house positions report high degrees of satisfaction, even though they have taken pay cuts.[68] An in-house attorney works for a company and provides advice on numerous legal matters. In-house attorneys working for large companies work in specialized departments on specific issues ranging form regulatory questions to contracts law to litigation issues. There are no billable hours to record, and the best perk of working in-house is that attorneys can turn to outside counsel, usually a law firm, that can help with complex legal questions. As such, these lawyers have better hours and more time for family. An in-house attorney is a part of a larger business organization and is part of a team.

The attorneys who stay in large firms remain in stiff competition for the next several years, hoping to win the brass ring. Most associates will not make partner. And after nine years as a law firm lawyer, job prospects will be quite difficult to find. What is worse, finding another job usually means taking a pay cut, even if they end up at another law firm willing to hire them. After all, what firm wants a senior associate who was passed over for partnership?

This will be the harsh reality if you don't make partner; and if you don't, or if you decide to leave law firm life at an earlier time in your career (i.e., before you're passed over for partner), you might say, "Well, I don't need to practice law, because I can do anything with a law degree."

CHAPTER NINE

THE NUMBER-ONE MYTH: YOU CAN DO ANYTHING WITH A LAW DEGREE

A dear (and brilliant) friend of mine graduated at the top of her class from a top law school but loathed the practice of law. She lasted eight months working for one of the top law firms in the country, then worked as a waitress while trying to figure out her next step. She married and started a family and is now earning a Master of Arts in Theology.

"You can do anything with a law degree" is a cliché, and the last time you will take this seriously is the day you enter law school.[69] You can't even *practice law* with a law degree! By this, I mean to say that number one, since jobs are scarce, competition is stiff and lawyers are a dime a dozen, it will be difficult to find a job after graduating from law school period, end of story. Number two, if you already have experience in transactional work, for instance, and want to continue to practice transactional law at another law firm or company, it will be difficult to find a job because of scarcity and competition. Number three, if you want to *switch* from transactional to litigation, you could pretty much forget about it, again because of scarcity and competition, and even worse, you will have been type cast.

Just like anything else, you'll have to have connections and have to give more than good reasons for any career change. No doubt, switching within the profession is easier than changing careers altogether. Also, bear in mind that you will have to take a salary cut and a demotion.

What are the practical benefits of a law degree? What are the benefits of working in a law firm? And where can it lead? The only groups who directly benefit from working in a law firm are those, which goes without saying, who actually make equity partner at a firm, those who go into their own practices, those who go into in-house practice, and those who have made connections in the business world and end up working for their clients. Practically, what lawyers are able to do are things within the legal profession—or in other professions—where they can use what they've learned.

If you decide to leave law firm life, your options will relate, to a certain degree, to the law. For instance, if you decide to teach, you will undoubtedly be teaching something about the law. Many lawyers go into politics; many lawyers go into legal recruiting for permanent and temporary placement agencies; and many others perform temporary and project work at firms.

Other than these options, there is little other practical application of a law degree. It makes no difference that you've got a fantastic education, great analytical abilities, and thinking that is as clear as a bell. So what? You will find that there are many, many other people with great experience in the field you realize you should have chosen years before. *Experience,* not a law degree, is the key. It will be difficult, at best, to change careers—unless you have connections, of course. Why would an employer hire a lawyer for a marketing job when other qualified and experienced individuals are seeking the same job? This is especially true in a down market.

During hard economic times, there are more available individuals in the market, and employers have the luxury of choosing the best among many, many people. There is no reason to choose a lawyer, unless the need is for someone to do legal work.

The attorneys who decide to return to school to get out of the law and change careers altogether are the ones who have taken a long and costly detour from where they should have been in the first place. For some, I suppose, this detour is a necessity; but it can be avoided with a little forethought and understanding of yourself.

A Word of Advice

Know Thyself.

—Unknown

Upon leaving one firm, I confided in several partners my dissatisfaction with law firm life. Each said to me the same thing: "I wish I had left while I had the chance. Now I can't because I have a wife, kids, responsibilities, and a certain lifestyle to maintain. It's just too late for me now. Leave while you can."

My suggestion is this: If you are in any way uncertain about practicing law, or if you have nothing else to do with your life and figure that you'll just go to law school, go to a firm as an intern first. Become a paralegal in real estate, corporate, tax, litigation, or in whichever practice area you believe you have an interest. Go and work in the business world. Go out in the real world and experiment *first*. You have the time now, and a year or two (or even more) will help you make a more educated, less costly decision. I know too many unhappy lawyers. Just review the stats. I would have to say that, other than the rainmaker partners, I have only met one lawyer at a large firm who truly liked it. She told me she loved it and that she actually felt like a lawyer. *I wonder what that feels like?* And so do most of the lawyers I know.

Law school is a huge expense, and you will be spending three years of your life in school again. These are years you could be spending exploring the practice of law itself from a "real-world" perspective. Or you could pursue more suitable possibilities for yourself. Ask yourself questions. What type of environment do you see yourself in? What type of people do you want to be around? Do you like research and writing? Do you like paperwork? Ask yourself as many questions as possible in order to narrow your scope. Go to your career counseling center.

Once you graduate from law school, perhaps, you will have to pay back student loans. The average debt after graduating from law school is $70,000.[70] This is an even greater expense if it only leads you to the discovery that you could have been spending your time and money training for something that you actually love doing. You may be surprised to discover that making a lot of money is not the most important consideration when facing a career choice. There is incomparable reward in living your life doing what you really want to do—and chances are, the money will follow. Of course, this talk about loving what you do does not apply to those who love money and nothing else; and if this is true, you should go into banking or become an entrepreneur—in any case, it does not mean you should be a lawyer.

If you simply want the education, and money isn't an object, then there's no good reason not to go to law school. If you know firsthand about the practice of law (perhaps, for example, your parents are lawyers), then you can also go with a certain level of confidence, free from illusions. If you have always dreamed about being a lawyer (and not because of all those glamorous TV shows), then you very well might have a good reason to go. If you are socially minded and truly desire to enter into politics or the public domain, or to work for non-profit organizations, then going to law school could be a good choice.

You should be 99% certain that you are truly passionate about the law. If you are passionate about it, you will most likely succeed in any area of the law and be fairly satisfied with your career choice. Better yet, knowing exactly *why* you are going to law school before you commit time and money to that endeavor will save you grief in the long run. You can do this by identifying a specific goal or genuine interest in an area that would benefit from a legal education.

Unfortunately, liking to argue or wanting to make the world a better place are not specific enough reasons. Not knowing what to do with your life is not a good enough reason to choose law either. Security certainly doesn't warrant the endeavor; as I'm sure you are aware, nothing is secure these days. In fact, more than 3,000 lawyers were laid off in the first quarter of 2009, and the number of unemployed lawyers jumped 66% to a ten-year high of 20,000.[71]

If a legal education is not useful to your specific goals, then going to law school will only slow you down. You may be surprised to discover that getting *out* of law is much more difficult than getting *in*. As an attorney, you will be so busy working all the time that you will not have the time to consider what else you want to do with your life. The years will just keep flying by. What is worse, you will not know how to do anything else; and most likely, the cost of change—tossing what you've gained and sacrificing income to learn something new—will be too high to allow a change, causing you to stay exactly where you are.

If you don't have the passion or certainty about the law, and you decide to go to law school anyway, simply to try to land any legal job, it is likely that you will end up leading a tolerable daily life—at best. This is especially true if you go to law school with the idea of making money at a big law firm, believing that financial reward will make up for the daily woes of big law firm life. Take note that practicing law is tedious and detail-oriented regardless of practice arena.

What is more, as elaborated on in Chapter Eight, lawyers who practice in any environment report being dissatisfied with the practice of law on some level. Granted, lawyers outside big law firm practice are not as dissatisfied as lawyers inside, but nonetheless, they are still dissatisfied.

CHAPTER TEN

MIGHT THE GLASS BE HALF-FULL?

Although my own hopes of finding a home at a major law firm did not work out long term, I realize that I have gained an invaluable education and experience in the real world. Low and behold, there is a positive side to going to law school and practicing law at a major firm!

For one thing, there is nothing like a law school education. This is for sure. Once you graduate, you will not be able to view the world in the same way that you did before you went to law school. This is not because you learn so much about the law per se, but because the way you think will be altered forever. The way you interpret things will be much more literal; and, unfortunately, at times, you will not be able to engage in simple conversation. Things that used to have simple meanings will suddenly have three different interpretations.

More importantly (despite all the secretarial tasks), you will learn the following while at a big law firm, which can only benefit you throughout your entire life:

- You will learn how to think and ask the right questions.
- You will learn how to cut to the chase.
- You will learn how to research and write skillfully.

- You will learn how to work under fire on a consistent basis so that most any other job will seem like a cake walk.
- You will learn about sophisticated transactions.
- You will deal with high-profile companies and clients.
- You will learn how to interact with people.
- You will learn about money.
- You will make some money.

Lastly, among all the printing, copying, and FedExing, you will discover the *practice* of law—something quite different from the law itself.

EPILOGUE

I hope that you found this book enlightening, especially if you are in the process of considering a job at a big law firm or seeking guidance in deciding about whether to attend law school for the purpose of practicing at a big law firm.

If you believe that you really want to go to law school to practice in another legal arena, outside the big law firm environment, I hope that you look beyond the scope of this book and do more research. Talk to people. Surf the Net. Find a summer job working in a firm or for a solo practitioner. In short, do what you need to do to learn more about the *reality* of practicing law firsthand. The time and money you will spend attending law school warrant an informed decision. Remember: Whatever you decide to do, you will be doing it every day of your life.

Each step of the journey is the journey.
—Zen Expression

APPENDICES

MARKET 2010 AND BEYOND

Headlines such as "Get Ready to Celebrate—Bonus News Is In," "Salaries at Largest Firms Up Again," and "Associate Bonuses Still Booming, Despite Salary Increase" have been superceded, and will continue to be for some time, by current headlines like "Big Law Firm Slashes All Associates' Pay," "Large Law Firms Cutting Pay for First-Year Attorneys," "Law Firm Cuts Keep on Coming," and "Recession Causing Layoffs at Big Firms." In other words, the party is over.

Partnerships are more difficult to attain than ever. In fact, more than forty firms made fewer partnership offers in 2009, and half intended to do so in 2010.[72] Further, more than one-quarter of firms de-equitized partners in 2009, and 36% intended to do so in 2010.[73] Finally, 14% of firms extended partnership track (the amount of time to make partner), and 20% intended to do so in 2010.[74]

In 2009, 64% of firms eliminated their summer programs, and 54% of firms did the same in 2010.[75] Firms also cut workforce. Sixty-seven percent of firms cut support staff (and intended to cut more in 2010), 43% cut paralegals, 44% cut associates, 25% cut partners, and 26% cut non-equity partners (and intended to cut more in 2010).[76] At the same time, however,

50% of all firms intended to increase lawyer head count in 2010.[77] In addition, firms intend to use more contract attorneys in the future. In 2009, 39% used contract attorneys, and in 2010, over 50% intended to use contract attorneys as well as making them apart of their permanent staffing needs.[78]

Top firms also cut salaries as much as 20%, and bonuses as much as 57%.[79] In addition, firms are revising their pay structures by decreasing salaries and bonuses and instituting pay freezes.[80]

In the beginning of 2008, landing a job at a firm was fairly fool-proof for qualified candidates; and now, during this time of economic turmoil, jobs are scarce. It is difficult to predict when the economy will stabilize and firms will start hiring in the hundreds again and whether salaries and bonuses will hit the highs of 2007 again in the near future—if ever.

You might say to yourself, however, that if you attend law school starting in 2011 and ride out the storm, by 2014 you should be able to land that dream job. But there is no predicting supply and demand levels after this severe contraction ends and the stabilization of the markets occurs. One thing is for sure, for the foreseeable future, there will be even less employment opportunities at major law firms than in the past.

NOTABLE STATISTICS[81]

- Median Starting Salaries for First-Year Associates by Firm Size 2009

    - 2-25 $70,000
    - 26-50 $92,500
    - 51-100 $104,000
    - 101-250 $110,00
    - 251+ $145,000

- Median Starting Salaries for Associates in Firms 251+ Lawyers –

    - Chicago, Los Angeles, New York
      and Washington, D.C. 2009 $160,000

- Average Profits Per Partner (PPP) and Compensation, 2009:[82]

    - Top 100 Average (PPP) $1,260,000
    - Top 100 Average Compensation $944,612
    - Top 10 High to Low
      (Average Compensation) $4,300,000–
                                     $2,120,000
    - Top 200 Average (PPP) $646,926[83]

- Total Associate Attrition Rate by Third Year: 38.3%

- Total Associate Attrition Rate by Fifth Year: 78%

- Associate Attrition Rates by Seventh Year:

  - Female   88%
  - Male   63%

- Partners:

  - Minorities   6.05%
  - Minority Female   1.88%
  - Female   19.21%
  - Male   79%

- Associates:

  - Minorities   19.67%
  - Minority Female   11.02%
  - Female   45.66%
  - Male   54.66%

- Openly Gay Partners and Associates:[84]

  - Partners   1.36%
  - Associates   2.29%

- Disabled Partners and Associates[85]

  - Partners   .22%
  - Associates   .17%

- Alcoholism:

  - General Population   10%
  - Attorneys

    - 2–20 years of practice   20%
    - \> 20 years of practice   25%

- Reporting of Major Depressive Disorder:

  Attorneys vs. Non-lawyers in Same Demographics   >3.6x

USEFUL RESOURCES

- Vault.com

  - A guide to law schools and law firms. Message boards and surveys detail insider views about firms and the practice of law. This site also has similar information for all industries.
  - http://www.vault.com/wps/portal/usa

- National Association for Lawyer Placement (NALP) and the NALP Foundation NALP.org

  - NALP is the premier resource for information on legal employment and recruiting.
  - http://www.nalp.org/

  - The NALP Foundation is a site devoted to industry research from employment and salary trends to legal task force suggestions for the legal field.
  - http://www.nalpfoundation.org/

- AmericanLawyer.com and Law.com

  - Excellent, extensive sites devoted to legal news, the latest information about law firms, and gossip.
  - http://www.nalpfoundation.org/
  - http://www.law.com/jsp/law/index.jsp

- Above the Law.com: A Legal Tabloid

  - Reporting news, gossip, and the legal profession's most colorful and powerful institutions.
  - http://abovethelaw.com/

- ABAnet.org: The American Bar Association

  - The site is primarily for law students and lawyers, providing information about the law and tools for career advancement. The site provides access to a variety of legal publications for purchase.
  - http://www.abanet.org/

NOTES

[1] Ronit Dinovitzer et al, NALP Foundation for Law Career and Research and Education (hereinafter NALP Foundation), "After the JD: First Results of a National Study in Legal Careers" (2004): Section 2, 19.

[2] Large law firms and major law firms as defined in this book are considered law firms with more than 50 lawyers with many different specialized practice groups, such as litigation, corporate, real estate, mergers and acquisitions, intellectual property, environmental and tax.

[3] Ronit Dinovitzer et al, NALP Foundation, "After the JD: First Results of a National Study in Legal Careers" (2004): Section 4, 34.

[4] Revised pages are more easily inserted (and old ones removed), and copies are more easily made, with the use of paper clips.

[5] Debra Cassens Weiss, "One Paper-Pushing Lawyer = Tons of Greenhouse Gases," ABA Journal – Law News Now, September 19, 2007, http://www.abajournal.com/news/article/one_paper_pushing_lawyer_tons_of_greenhouse_gases/

[6] Peter Lattman, "Does 'Thank You' Help Keep Associates?" *The Wall Street Journal*, January 24, 2007, B7.

[7] David Lat, "Sullivan & Cromwell: Because Charney v. S&C Is Just the Tip of the Iceberg," *Above the Law.com, A Legal Tabloid,* January 25, 2007, http://abovethelaw.com/2007/01/charney_v_sc_a_kinder_gentler.php.

[8] National Association for Law Placement (hereinafter NALP),"How Much Do Associates Work? Most Firms Do Not Require 2,000 Billable Hours," NALP *Bulletin,* April, 2009, http://www.nalp.org/may07billablehrs

[9] Ibid. More specifically, in 2007, for firms with 50 or fewer attorneys, total hours worked were 1,963, with 1,814 billed; for firms with 51–100 attorneys, total hours worked were 1,984, with 1,831 hours billed; for

firms with 101–250 attorneys, total hours worked were 2,023, with 1,831 billed; for firms with 251–500 attorneys, total hours worked were 2,112, with 1,858 billed; for firms with 501–700 attorneys, total hours worked were 2,119, with 1,826 billed; for firms with 701-plus attorneys, total hours worked were 2,172, with 1,847 hours billed. Note that 2008 hours were slightly less due to the economic downturn. NALP, "A Look at Associates Hours and at Law Firm Pro Bono Programs," NALP *Bulletin*, April 2010, http://www.nalp.org/july2009hoursandprobono

[10] Ibid. The billable requirement for 50 or fewer attorneys being 1,814 hours and for firms 701-plus attorneys, 1,938 hours, with firms with 51–700 attorneys falling between.

[11] Ibid.

[12] Taking the average salary of lawyers, out of 251 lawyers or more, and dividing that number by the average number of hours worked for firms equaling 251 lawyers or more, (130,000k/2,134 hrs.). Figures obtained from, "How Much Do Associates Work?" NALP *Bulletin*, April, 2009, and "How Much Do Law Firms Pay Associates? A 14-Year Retrospective as Reported by Firms," NALP *Bulletin*, September, 2009, http://www.nalp.org/may07billablehrs and http://www.nalp.org/2009septnewassocsalaries

[13] NALP, "Most Lawyers Working Part-time Are Women—Overall Number of Lawyers Working Part-time Remains Small" December 17, 2009, Press Release, http://www.nalp.org/parttimesched2009

[14] Angela Cheng, "Part-Time Culture Grows at Firms," *The National Law Journal*, October 26, 2004, http://www.law.com/jsp/article.jsp?id=1098608713720.

[15] Elie Mystal, "Are Contract Attorneys Getting Blacklisted?" *Above the Law*, June 23, 2010, http://abovethelaw.com/2010/06/are-contract-attorneys-getting-blacklisted/

[16] Note that these figures are based on pre-economic collapse. Rates for specialization projects dropped as low as half post-economic collapse in 2008.

[17] Ibid. Rates dropped to as low as $20.00 per hour.

[18] Stephanie Francis Ward, "The Ultimate Time–Money Trade-Off?" *ABA J. EReport,* February, 2007, http://abajournal.com/magazine/the_ultimate_time_money_trade_off1/.

[19] Aric Press and Greg Mulligan , "Lessons of the Am Law 100," *The American Lawyer.com*, May 1, 2010. The stability of profit per partner over the previous year is attributed to a reduction in expenses, layoffs and deferrals and decrease in the number of equity partners themselves. http://www.law.com/jsp/article.jsp?id=1202454891802

[20] Alison Frankel, "American Law 100: Veil of Tiers," *The American Lawyer,* 2004, http://www.abanet.org/yld/summits/veil_of_tiers.pdf

[21] Ibid.

[22] Neil Solomon, "Figuring the Odds of Making Partner: Timing the Market," *National Law Journal,* July 16, 2002, http://www.law.com/jsp/nlj/PubArticleNLJ.jsp?id=900005531189

[23] NALP, "New Findings on Salaries for Public Interest Attorneys," NALP *Bulletin*, September, 2008, http://www.nalp.org/2008sepnewfindings

[24] NALP, "How Much Do Law Firms Pay New Associates? A 14-Year Retrospective as Reported by Firms," NALP *Bulletin*, September 2009, http://www.nalp.org/2009septnewassocsalaries

[25] NALP, "Salaries at Largest Firms Up Again," August 21, 2008, Press Release, http://www.nalp.org/salariesatlargestfirmsupagain

[26] Ibid.

[27] Ibid.

[28] Ibid.

[29] Nathan Koppel, "Get Ready to Celebrate—Bonus News Is In," *The Wall Street Journal, Law Bog*, December 8, 2006, http://blogs.wsj.com/law/2006/12/08/2902/.

[30] Susie Potier, "2007: The Year in Bonuses—Winners and Losers," *The Glass Hammer*, December 19, 2007, http://www.theglasshammer.com/news/2007/12/19/2007-the-year-in-bonuses—winners-and-losers/

[31] Cynthia L. Spanhel, NALP Foundation, "Toward Effective Management of Associate Mobility: A Status Report on Attrition," 2005: 21.

[32] Ibid.

[33] Ibid. Blacks, Asians and Hispanics are more likely than whites to be working in government and not–for-profit organizations, Ronit Dinovitzer et al, NALP Foundation, "After the JD: First Results of a National Study in Legal Careers" (2004): Section 9, 64.

[34] American Bar Association, "First Year and Total J.D. Enrollment by Gender, 1947–2005," 2008, http://www.abanet.org/legaled/statistics/charts/stats%20-%206.pdf

[35] NALP, "Law Firm Diversity Demographics Show Little Change, Despite Economic Downturn," October 21, 2009, Press Release, http://www.nalp.org/oct09lawfirmdiversity

[36] Emily Barker, "Engendering Change," *The American Lawyer*, June, 2003.

[37] NALP, "Law Firm Diversity Demographics Show Little Change, Despite Economic Downturn," October 21, 2009, Press Release, http://www.nalp.org/oct09lawfirmdiversity

[38] Mona Harrington and Helen Hsi, "Women Lawyers and Obstacles to Leadership," *MIT Workplace Center*, Spring (2007) 13, http://web.mit.edu/workplacecenter/docs/law-report_4-07.pdf

[39] Ibid.

[40] Ibid.

[41] NALP Foundation, "After the JD: First Results of a National Study in Legal Careers," 2004: 60.

[42] Ibid.

[43] Joanne Cronrath Bamberger, "Where's the Class of '88?" *Legal Times,* September 22, 2004.

[44] Ibid.

[45] National Association of Women Lawyers, "Report of the Third Annual National Survey on Retention and Promotion of Women in Law Firm," November, 2008: 14, http://www.starneslaw.com/pdf/NAWL_2008_Survey_Report_FINAL.pdf

[46] Leigh Jones, "Toughest Case Is Making Partner," *The National Law Journal*, August 31, 2005, http://www.law.com/jsp/article.jsp?id=1125392710244.

[47] Timothy L. O'Brien, "Why Do So Few Women Reach the Top of Big Law Firms?" *The New York Times*, Business Section, March 19, 2006, http://www.nytimes.com/2006/03/19/business/yourmoney/19law.html

[48] Cynthia L. Spanhel, NALP, "Toward Effective Management of Associate Mobility: A Status Report on Attrition," (2005) 16.

[49] Cynthia L. Spanhel, NALP Foundation, "Toward Effective Management of Associate Mobility: A Status Report on Attrition," (2005) 21. For law firms with 251 – 500 lawyers, the attrition rate reached 63.2% by the 55th month of employment, and 43.1% by the 40th month, and the attrition rate for firms with more than 500 lawyers was 46.7% by the 55th month and 29.5% by the 40th month, Paula A. Patton, NALP Foundation, "Keeping the Keepers II Mobility and Management of Associates" (2003) 22, 33.

[50] NALP Foundation, "Keeping the Keepers II: Mobility and Management of Associates," *Executive Summary* (2003), http://www.nalpfoundation.org/keepingthekeepersii

[51] Brian J. Ritchey, "Associate Attrition Skyrockets by Year 5," *LexisNexis*, June 18, 2008, http://www.lexisnexis.com/COMMUNITY/REDWOODANALYTICS/blogs/morepartnerincome/archive/2008/06/18/associate-attrition-skyrockets-by-year-5.aspx

[52] Mona Harrington and Helen Hsi, "Women Lawyers and Obstacles to Leadership," *MIT Workplace Center*, Spring (2007): 12–14.

[53] Ibid.

[54] Ibid.

[55] Ibid.

[56] Ibid, Section 6: 48, 50.

[57] Ronit Dinovitzer and Bryant G. Garth, "Lawyer Satisfaction in the Process of Structuring Legal Careers," *Law and Society Review* 41 (2007): 22.

[58] Ronit Dinovitzer et al, NALP Foundation, "After the JD: First Results of a National Study in Legal Careers," (2004) Section 6: 47. Blacks report the highest level of satisfaction with their decision, with Hispanics ranking almost as high, Section 9: 64.

[59] Brian Melendez, ABA Young Lawyers Division Survey: Career Satisfaction. (2000): 32, http://new.abanet.org/marketresearch/Pages/StatisticalResources.aspx

[60] Heather Sokoloff, "Legal Exodus," *National Post*, March 17, 2005, FP3.

[61] Rick B. Allen, "Alcoholism, Drug Abuse and Lawyers: Are We Ready to Address the Denial?" *Creighton Law Review,* Vol. 31, No. 7 265–266 (1997).

[62] C. Patrick Schiltz, "Those Unhappy, Unhealthy Lawyers," *Notre Dame Magazine*, Autumn, 1999.

[63] Ben W. Heinman Jr. and David B. Wilkins "Big Firm Associates: Why They Go and How to Keep Them," February 29, 2008, http://www.law.com/jsp/article.jsp?id=900005560463

[64] Dan Slater, "Another View: In Praise of Law Firm Layoffs," *The New York Times*, July 1, 2009, http://dealbook.blogs.nytimes.com/2009/07/01/another-view-in-praise-of-law-firm-layoffs/.

[65] The Snark, "Layoffs, What Layoffs?" *Fulton County Daily Record*, March 12, 2009, http://www.law.com/jsp/article.jsp?id=1202428987506.

[66] Vivia Chen, "White & Case: Waiting for the Axe to Fall 400 Times," *The American Lawyer*, March 11, 2009, http://www.law.com/jsp/law/careercenter/lawArticleCareerCenter.jsp?id=1202428954834

[67] NALP Foundation, "Keeping the Keepers II: Mobility and Management of Associates (1998–2003)," *Executive Summary*, 2003 and NALP Foundation, "Beyond the Bidding Wars: A Survey of Associate Attrition, Departure Destinations, and Workplace Incentives," *Executive Summary*, 2003, http://www.nalpfoundation.org/keepingthekeepersii

[68] Katheryn Hayes Tucker, "Firm Lawyers Jump Ship for Quality of Life In-House," *Fulton County Daily Report*, July 27, 2007. Source: http://www.law.com/jsp/ihc/PubArticleIHC.jsp?id=1185482031458 http://www.law.northwestern.edu/career/markettrends/2007/qss16khy.pdf

[69] Mark L. Byers and Ronald W. Fox. "Taking Control Over Your Career and Your Life: Through the Looking Glass-Your Options in the Law," *Find Law, for Legal Professionals,*http://profdev.lp.findlaw.com/column/column5.html.

[70] Ibid.

[71] Jesse J. Holland, "Recession Causing Lawyer Layoffs at Big Firms," *Associated Press*, April 13, 2009, Retrieved from http://a.abcnews.com/Politics/wireStory?id=7325602.

[72] Thomas S. Clay and Eric A. Seeger. "Law Firms in Transition 2010." An Altman Weil Flash Survey, *Summary,* 2010, http://www.altmanweil.com/index.cfm/fa/r.resource_detail/oid/6ddd4b8a-88a3-44ef-85a1-5a9a7ce501ac/resource/New_Law_Firm_Survey_A_Consensus_on_Change.cfm

[73] Ibid.

[74] Ibid.

[75] Ibid.

[76] Ibid. *see also*, The American Lawyer.com, "The Layoff List," http://www.law.com/jsp/tal/PubArticleTAL.jsp?id=1202425647706&slreturn=1&hbxlogin=1

[77] Ibid.

[78] Ibid.

[79] Carlyn Kolker, "Law Firms Slash First-Year Pay," *Bloomberg,* December 23, 2009, http://www.bloomberg.com/apps/news?pid=newsarchive&sid=akMUcQT.C_Nk

[80] Dan Slater, "At Law Firms Reconsidering the Model for Associates' Pay," *The New York Times, Deal Book*, April 1, 2010, http://dealbook.blogs.nytimes.com/2010/04/01/at-law-firms-reconsidering-the-model-for-associates-pay/

[81] The various statistical references have already been cited elsewhere throughout this book unless otherwise provided.

[82] American Lawyer.com, "The Am Law 100 2010," May 1, 2010, http://www.law.com/jsp/tal/PubArticleTAL.jsp?id=1202448485189

[83] The American Lawyer.com, "The Am Law 200 2010," June 1, 2010, http://www.law.com/jsp/tal/PubArticleTAL.jsp?id=1202458243145&slreturn=1&hbxlogin=1

[84] NALP, "Although Most Firms Collect GLBT Lawyer Information, Overall Numbers Remain Low," NALP *Bulletin*, December 2009, http://www.nalp.org/dec09glbt

[85] NALP, "Law Firms Report More GLBT Lawyers, But Numbers Remain Small," NALP *Bulletin*, November, 2008, http://www.nalp.org/moreglbtlawyers

www.ingramcontent.com/pod-product-compliance
Lightning Source LLC
Chambersburg PA
CBHW022111170526
45157CB00004B/1575